BUG

Bites

priddy books

WHAT IS A BUG?

Bug, insect, or mini-beast—these are the **words** used to describe the **different** types of **creepy-crawly** you will find inside this book. There are many different groups of **bugs**. Read on to **find** out more. . . .

INSECT

Thorax
Head

Abdomen

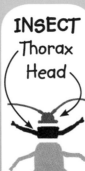

Spiders and scorpions are arachnids.

They have eight legs and no wings.

Insects have three sections to their bodies, six legs, and usually have wings.

Bugs are a special kind of insect with a sucking mouth.

Centipedes and millipedes are myriapods.

They have lots of body sections and lots of legs.

Pillbugs are crustaceans,

just like crabs.

And worms, slugs, and snails. . . .

are not bugs at all, because they have soft bodies and no legs. But they are creepy and slimy mini-beasts, so they have a special place in this book.

When you see this sign, it's a. . . .

REAL-SIZE BUG

Real-size bugs

Amazingly, there are more bugs in the world than any other type of animal. Some bugs are so tiny, we don't often see them. But some bugs are so **big**, we can't FAIL to notice them. And you're about to meet them, in **real size!**

QUEEN ALEXANDRA'S BIRDWING

The **Queen Alexandra's birdwing** is the **largest** butterfly in the **world**. The females can have a **wingspan** over 11 inches. The males are slightly **smaller** but still huge!

Actual size of a male: width 10 in

Female

1

Find the bug sticker on every fact page!

REAL-SIZE BUG

The male is the most beautiful, with shimmering green, blue, and black wings and a yellow body.

4

Eggs

Caterpillar

Pupa

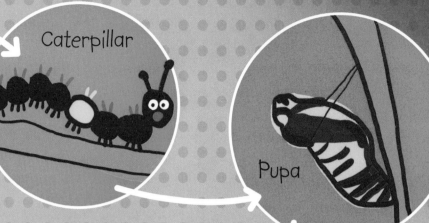

Butterflies are shape-shifters. They change from an egg to a caterpillar to a pupa, then they emerge as an adult butterfly.

Phew! What a journey.

They were named after the wife of King Edward VII of Great Britain.

Back off, birdy! I'm REALLY poisonous.

As caterpillars, they eat poisonous pipevine leaves, which makes them extremely deadly to predators.

FACT FILE

Claim to bug fame:
The biggest butterfly

How big?
Over 11 inches wide

What does it eat?
Flower nectar

Watch out. . . . **It's poisonous, (but only to birds and other bugs).**

Endangered?
Yes. Farming and logging are destroying its rainforest home.

Where in the world?
Papua New Guinea

ATLAS MOTH

The **Atlas moth** is one of the giants of the moth world. It has **huge** wings, but its hairy **body** is tiny in comparison! Females **wings** can span up to 12 inches—try measuring that with a ruler!

REAL-SIZE BUG

Feathery antennae, or feelers, on its head

Because they are so large, the discarded cocoons of the moth are sometimes used as purses in Taiwan!

The wingtips look like snakes' heads to scare predators away.

Actual size of a male: width 9 in

As caterpillars, these moths eat loads! They grow quickly, until they are plump and almost 5 inches long. Then caterpillars spins silk cocoons and turn into moths.

BURP!

2

Once Atlas moths have emerged from their cocoons, they only live for two weeks. This is because they have no mouths, so are unable to eat. These moths can only survive on the fat stores they build up as caterpillars.

R.I.P.

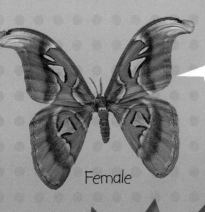

Female

What's wrong with me?

Although females is bigger, they are not as beautiful as the male!

It is thought that these moths are named Atlas after the maplike pattern on their wings.

FACT FILE

Claim to bug fame:
The biggest moth

How big?
The females can grow to 12 inches wide.

What does it eat?
As an adult moth, it doesn't!
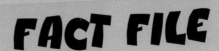

Watch out. . . . **It's going to die soon!**

Endangered?
No

Where in the world?
Southeast Asia

THE WORLD'S STRONGEST BUG

Dung beetle

DID YOU KNOW?
The dung beetle moves balls of dung with its back legs to feed its young.

SIZE: Average 2 in

DIET: Dung (poop), mushrooms, decaying leaves, fruit

FROM: Found all over the world, except Antarctica

SPECIAL SKILLS: It uses the stars to navigate its way home with its dung balls.

POO! What a stink!

DID YOU KNOW?

There are four types: the tiny minims, the workers, the soldiers, and the queen.

Leafcutter ant

One of these bugs can pull 1,141 times its own body weight. The other can pull 50 times. They are both stronger than the world's strongest human, who can only pull 23 times his own body weight.

SIZE: 0.5 in

DIET: Fungi, leaf sap

FROM: South and Central America, Mexico, southern states of the USA

SPECIAL SKILLS: Leafcutter ants have very powerful jaws—they vibrate over a thousand times a second to slice off pieces of leaves.

BOTH BUGS CAN CARRY LOTS OF STUFF, BUT WHO IS THE WINNER IN THIS BUG BATTLE?
TURN TO PAGE 54 TO FIND OUT!

BUG HUNT

Head out to your yard or park and look for these bugs! Check the boxes when you find them and draw a picture of what you see.

Worm

Check the box when you find me!

A great place to find a bug is under stones, logs, or leaves.

Ladybug

Check the box when you find me!

Bumblebee

Check the box when you find me!

Butterfly

Check the box
when you find me!

Why not try looking in flowers or bushes, too?

 # Spider

Check the box
when you find me!

 # Ant

Check the box
when you find me!

 # Pillbug

Check the box
when you find me!

Make sure
to ask an adult
to help you.

TARANTULA HAWK WASP

The **Tarantula hawk wasp** has a **body** that's 1.5 inches long. With its **wings** and legs, this makes it the size of a **small hand**! Tarantula hawks are so-called because they like to pick **fights** with **tarantula** spiders—and they often **win!**

Yellow and orange wings

REAL-SIZE BUG

Actual size: 1.5 in

They have long antennae, and males' are more tightly curved than females'.

Long black legs with hooked claws

The female searches the ground for unlucky tarantulas. Once found, she uses her sting to paralyze the spider. The female then lays an egg on the spider's body, before dragging it to an underground burrow and burying it alive!

She said come home for dinner!

When the wasp's eggs have hatched into young larvae (grubs), they start to feed on the spider from the inside until it is well and truly dead!

I want to be alone!

Most wasps like to live together in groups called colonies, but the tarantula hawk is happier alone!

Help the honeybee
find its way through the
maze to the sunflower.

Start

Finish

GIANT WATER BUG

The **Giant water bug** is one of the most **gruesome** predators of the bug world. This **ferocious** bug lies at the bottom of freshwater pools, waiting for its **prey**, or an **unlucky** foot, to come close.

If threatened, the Giant water bug plays dead and releases a sticky fluid from its bottom. Gross!

Actual size, length: 5 in

5

Powerful front legs to grab other bugs and prey

REAL-SIZE BUG

Piercing, sucking mouth

Once the water bug has ambushed its prey, it injects its victims with a powerful saliva which melts it from the inside out. Then, it feasts on the victim by sucking out its liquefied remains. Tasty!

Giant water bugs are good dads! They carry their offspring as eggs on their wings until they are ready to hatch.

In Southeast Asia, Giant water bugs are a popular snack, and are said to taste like liquorice and scrambled eggs!

While not fatal to humans, the Giant water bug's bite is one of the most painful on Earth.

The Giant water bug has some interesting nicknames, including Toe-biter, Electric-light bug, and Alligator tick.

OUCH!

FACT FILE

Claim to bug fame:
Most gruesome predator

How big?
The largest of the species can grow up to 5 inches.

What does it eat?
Fish, frogs, and larger pond life, including baby turtles and watersnakes!

Watch out. . . . **They bite your toes!**

Endangered?
No

Where in the world?
Freshwater ponds and streams in North America, South America, Northern Australia, and Southeast Asia

GOLIATH BEETLE

The **Goliath beetle** is the big daddy of beetles. It is also one of the **heaviest** insects in the **world** in its larval stage (like a caterpillar). The adult beetles are **lighter**, but they are a real handful—literally!

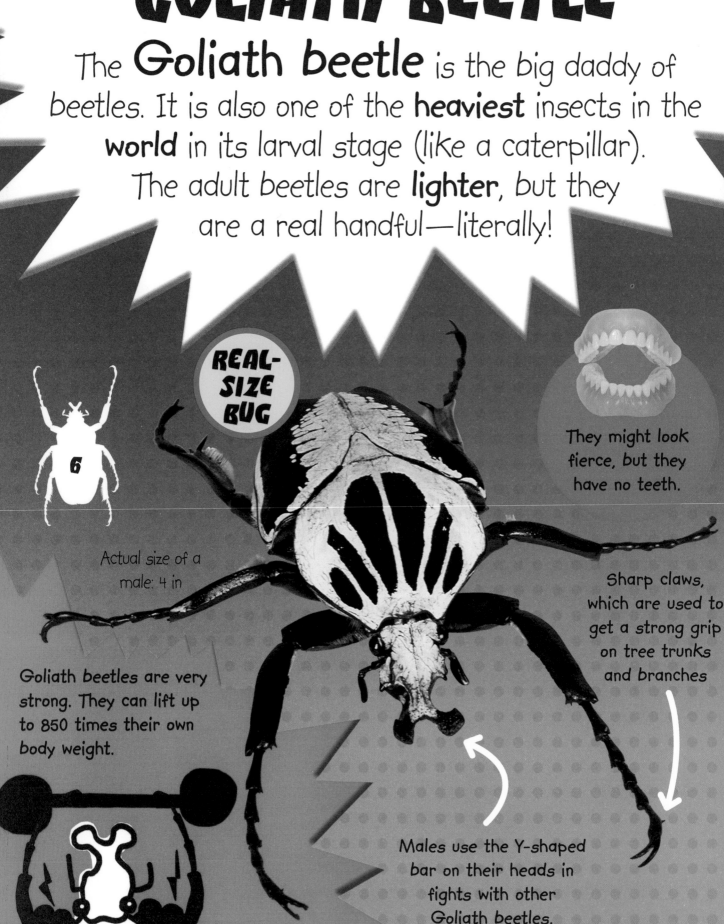

REAL-SIZE BUG

They might look fierce, but they have no teeth.

Actual size of a male: 4 in

Sharp claws, which are used to get a strong grip on tree trunks and branches

Goliath beetles are very strong. They can lift up to 850 times their own body weight.

Males use the Y-shaped bar on their heads in fights with other Goliath beetles.

Grr!

You can see its second pair of wings when it flies.

Despite being heavy, the Goliath beetle can still fly. It has a hard outer set of wings that protects a second set of flying wings underneath.

FACT FILE

Claim to bug fame:
The heaviest beetle

How big?

The males can grow over 4 inches long.

What does it eat?
Tree sap, ripe fruit

Watch out. . . . **It's big!**

Endangered?
No

Where in the world?
Africa

Is it a bird? Is it a plane? No, it's Superbeetle!

Although primarily vegetarian in the wild, Goliath beetles in captivity are known to enjoy gobbling up cat or dog food!

THE MOST VENOMOUS BUG

DID YOU KNOW?
The Red-kneed tarantula has big fangs and can rear up to look really threatening.

Red-kneed tarantula

SIZE: Up to 6 in

DIET: Insects and other bugs

FROM: Mexico

SPECIAL SKILLS: The female tends to be more aggressive than the male.

These guys should come with a warning!

Black widow spider

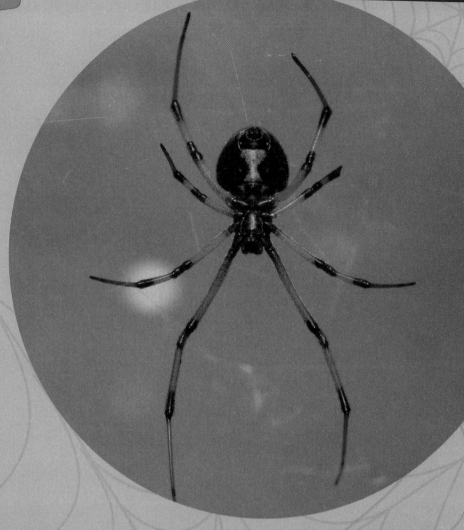

DID YOU KNOW?
The Black Widow has a distinctive red hourglass shape on its body.

SIZE: Up to 1.5 in (females)

DIET: Insects

FROM: Mostly USA, similar kinds in South America, Australia (redback), Africa (button spider), and Southern Asia

SPECIAL SKILLS: They are considered to be the most venomous spiders in North America.

Not sure this is a hotel!

BOTH SPIDERS PACK A LOT OF VENOM, BUT WHICH ONE WINS THIS BUG BATTLE?
TURN TO PAGE 54 TO FIND OUT!

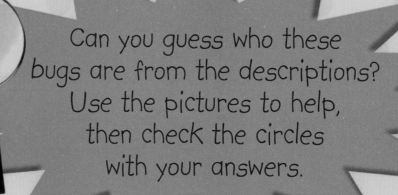

Can you guess who these bugs are from the descriptions? Use the pictures to help, then check the circles with your answers.

1. I have a long, thin, colorful body, see-through wings, and like to fly close to the water. Who am I?

a) a fly ⚪ b) a dragonfly ⚪ c) a butterfly ⚪

2. I'm a noisy green or brown bug with long legs that can also jump really high! Who am I?

a) a cockroach ⚪ b) a grasshopper ⚪ c) a Goliath beetle ⚪

DID YOU KNOW?
Ladybugs may look cute, but they are known to eat each other. Yuck!

3. I am usually red with black spots, but I can also be yellow with spots, and am able to fly. Who am I?

a) an ant

b) an earwig

c) a ladybug

○ ○ ○

DID YOU KNOW?
There are almost 2,000 species of scorpions. That's a BIG family!

4. I have eight legs, a furry body, and venomous fangs. Who am I?

a) a tarantula

b) a scorpion

c) a bee

○ ○ ○

TURN TO PAGE 56 TO FIND THE ANSWERS!

NATURE TRAIL

Get ready to go exploring!
Which of these bugs will you find?

- BUTTERFLY — Meadows, parks, and gardens
- CATERPILLAR — On leaves and stems of plants and trees
- GRASSHOPPER, OR CRICKET — Meadows, fields, and long grasses
- BEE — Meadows, parks, and gardens
- BEETLE — Undergrowth in parks, woods, and gardens
- LADYBUG — Gardens, forests, fields, and grassland
- ANT — Everywhere—look for anthills or around logs
- WORM — Underground, in mud, soil, or compost
- SNAIL OR SLUG — On the ground (especially on damp days), on fences, among vegetables
- EARWIG — Undergrowth in parks, woods, and gardens
- APHID — On the stems of young plants and flowers
- FLY — Everywhere—look in your house
- PILLBUG — Under plant pots and old bark
- DRAGONFLY — Usually near water
- SPIDER — Everywhere—check your shed

Use your senses

Use your ears as well as your eyes.

WHAT YOU WILL NEED

Before you go out on your nature trail, find these things, and take an adult!

Make sure to check the weather and go prepared!

Magnifying glass

Notebook, and if you have it, a bug book, to take with you

Backpack

Plastic gloves

Clear container to study your bugs more closely

Pencils

Write your observations here ....

....

....

....

....

....

....

....

....

....

....

....

GIANT WETA

What's a **Giant weta**? It's like a cricket, only much bigger. This **weird-looking** bug is **endangered** due to predators such as rats and is now found only in **New Zealand.**

7

Actual size of the average giant weta: body length 4 in

REAL-SIZE BUG

Most wetas have ears on their knees. They pick up vibrations around them, especially the chirps of other wetas.

Pardon?

Ugly? Me?

There are many species of weta. They all live in New Zealand where the native Maoris called them "weta punga." This is often translated as "god of ugly things."

The Giant weta is so big and heavy, unlike other types of weta, it is unable to jump!

Don't worry, neither can I!

FACT FILE

Claim to bug fame:
One of the heaviest insects, maybe the heaviest

How big?
Females can grow up to 8 inches

What does it eat?
Leaves, buds, flowers, fruits

Watch out. . . . **They sometimes bite and scratch, but they aren't harmful.**

Endangered?
Yes

Where in the world?
New Zealand

A female was discovered on an island near New Zealand that weighed as much as three mice! She may have been the world's heaviest insect!

How old?!

Wetas are so old, they were around with the dinosaurs, which was millions of years ago!

GIANT BURROWING COCKROACH

Insects **don't** get much creepier or crawlier than the cockroach. But the **Giant burrowing cockroach** is around four times **larger** than the **common** species. Yikes!

The Giant burrowing cockroach is also known as the Litter bug or Rhinoceros cockroach.

Unlike some other cockroaches, they don't have wings so are unable to fly.

Huh?!

Say what?!

8

REAL-SIZE BUG

Actual size: 3 in

They can grow as big as your hand.

This cockroach lives underground in the forests of Queensland, Australia, coming out at night for food.

Who needs wings underground?!

FACT FILE

Claim to bug fame:
One of the biggest, heaviest cockroaches

How big?
3 inches long

What does it eat?
Dry woodland leaves

Watch out. . . . **It's big, but harmless and doesn't spread disease like other roaches.**

Endangered?
No

Where in the world?
Australia

That's a lot of diapers.

They also don't lay eggs, which is REALLY unusual for an insect. Instead they have *baby* burrowing cockroaches, sometimes thirty at a time!

The Giant burrowing cockroach has an even *bigger* relative, the Central American giant cockroach.

Hola! I'm Blaberus giganteus.

Surprisingly, this cockroach makes a really great pet!

Females can reach 4 in long!

THE SMELLIEST BUG

Stink bug

SIZE: Up to 0.6 in

DIET: Fruit, leaves, vegetables

FROM: There are stink bug species on almost every continent.

SPECIAL SKILLS: It produces a foul odor from under its body when threatened or squashed.

I think I'm in love!!

DID YOU KNOW?
Its smell is said to be a bit like sweaty feet. Disgusting!

Bombardier beetle

DID YOU KNOW?
The beetle lays its eggs in decaying plants or animal carcasses.

SIZE: Up to 0.7 in

DIET: Insects

FROM: Most warm areas

SPECIAL SKILLS: It sprays a foul-smelling hot liquid out of its bottom!

BOTH USE THEIR SUPER-SMELLY ODORS AS A FORM OF DEFENSE, BUT WHICH IS THE SMELLIEST?
TURN TO PAGE 54 TO FIND OUT!

MIX AND MATCH

Can you find the stickers and match the pairs of bugs?

9

Snail

10

Ladybug

Scorpion

Tarantula

11

Earwig

Atlas moth

How **many** of these bugs have **wings?**

Which **bug** has eight **legs?**

13

Tarantula

12

Atlas moth

Earwig

Butterfly

Snail

14

Scorpion

I'm so pretty!

15

Butterfly

Ladybug

33

GOLIATH BIRD-EATING SPIDER

The **Goliath bird-eating spider** is a **giant** of the spider world. It may be the biggest and **heaviest** tarantula, and has **fangs** sharper than a **cheetah's claws**.

Actual size: body length over 4.5 in; leg span up to 12 in

FACT FILE

Claim to bug fame:
One of the world's largest spiders

How big?
Up to 12 inches wide, including its legs

What does it eat?
Mostly insects, rats, mice, worms, and frogs: sometimes a baby bird (but that's rare).

Watch out. . . . It can bite you, but it is not deadly to humans.

Endangered?
At risk

Where in the world?
South America's rainforests

Goliaths don't often bite humans. Their first form of defense is to flick tiny hairs from their body. This might not sound dangerous, but if the hairs get into your nose, eyes, or throat, they can be very irritating.

And I'm not afraid to use it!

Sensitive
hairs on legs

Eight eyes

REAL-
SIZE
BUG

Happy
Birthday

Goliath spiders
can live up to
30 years.

In South America, some
people actually eat roasted
tarantulas! REALLY!

Despite having eight
eyes, these spiders
have poor eyesight.
To make up for this,
when hunting prey they
sense movement by
picking up vibrations
using hairs on their legs.

EMPEROR SCORPION

The **Emperor scorpion** is one of the **largest** scorpions in the world, growing over 7 inches in length. It has two large **pincers** and a stinger on its **tail**, but it is not as **venomous** or **aggressive** as other scorpions.

The Emperor scorpion is shy and not naturally aggressive—it will only sting you as a defense mechanism!

Termites are this scorpion's main food source. They are able to dig as far down as 6 feet to find termite nests.

REAL-SIZE BUG

Actual size: body length up to 7.5 in

Emperors have strong pincers and can give you a nasty nip.

Eight legs like a spider

Emperors are kept as pets by scorpion lovers because of their calm nature and lower levels of toxic venom.

STINGER

Who'd want a dog?

The Emperor scorpion has a special trick—it is able to glow under UV light! It may be a chemical reaction, or to lure prey. No one really knows!

Emperors are good mothers! They give birth to live babies, which are born white. They climb onto Mom's back for protection as soon as they are born.

FACT FILE

Claim to bug fame:
The largest scorpion (not the longest)

How big?
Over 7.5 inches long

What does it eat?
Mostly insects

Watch out. . . . **It can sting you, and it can nip you.**

Endangered?
The pet trade is causing concern for the species.

Where in the world?
West Africa

THE HIGHEST JUMPER

DID YOU KNOW?
The flea can jump up to 8 inches high: up to 150 times its own height!

Cat flea

Wheeee!

SIZE: Average 0.2 in

DIET: Blood

FROM: Worldwide

SPECIAL SKILLS: Their jumping ability helps them leap from animal to animal.

Froghopper (Spittlebug)

SIZE: Average 0.3 in

DIET: Plants

FROM: Worldwide

SPECIAL SKILL:
Their jumping ability
helps them leap
from plant to plant
and away from enemies.

DID YOU KNOW?
The spittlebug is well
known for the froth it
produces to hide its
nymphs (babies).
It's often called
cuckoo spit.

Nothing to
do with me!

SO WHICH OF THESE TWO ATHLETIC BUGS WINS THE HIGH-JUMP BUG BATTLE?
TURN TO PAGE 55 TO FIND OUT!

Are you a budding entomologist, or an insect expert? In each group of mini-beasts, one is NOT an insect. Can you circle each one? **WATCH OUT** for the trick question!

Don't forget, insects have three sections to their body, six legs, and often have wings.

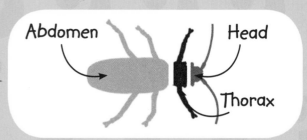

Abdomen   Head

Thorax

1. a) a grasshopper   b) a spider   c) a katydid

2. a) a centipede   b) an ant   c) a wasp

3. a) a pillbug   b) a stink bug   c) a ladybug

4.   a) a fly   b) an earwig   c) a snail

5.   a) a beetle   b) a cockroach   c) a scorpion

6.   a) a termite   b) a worm   c) a caterpillar

7.   a) a mosquito   b) a bee   c) a flea

8.   a) a dragonfly   b) a bat   c) a butterfly

Answers on page 56!

Can you see all the creepy crawly names in the word search? There are 10 bugs to find!

b	u	t	t	e	r	f	l	y	e
a	y	s	a	a	m	k	t	a	a
r	e	x	n	e	i	d	w	n	r
e	b	e	t	a	o	r	a	c	w
s	e	o	i	o	i	x	s	c	i
p	e	y	m	t	e	l	p	o	g
i	y	l	s	r	e	m	t	u	f
d	a	f	l	e	a	h	o	r	l
e	q	e	t	h	u	e	n	t	e
r	c	z	s	l	u	g	a	m	h

flea   snail   earwig   spider   wasp

bee   ant   butterfly   moth   slug

43

AFRICAN LAND SNAIL

This **big land snail** grows to almost 8 inches in length. Its **shell** grows as the snail **grows**, and it is the perfect thing to **protect** the snail from **birds** and other predators.

Snails are not insects. They are molluscs, just like slugs and octopuses. The things they have in common are soft bodies and no legs, though they do have a foot to help them get around!

Its shell is a shaped like a cone and is very tall.

Muscular foot oozes slime

18

Actual size: length 8 in

REAL-SIZE BUG

A snail produces slime. This is amazingly sticky, shiny stuff that helps it move, protects its body, and enables it to slide up walls!

FACT FILE

Claim to bug fame:
The largest land snail

How big?
Up to 8 inches long

What does it eat?
Plants, fruits, vegetables

Watch out.... **They can't hurt humans, but they can eat a lot of crops.**

Endangered?
No

Where in the world?
Originally East Africa, but have spread

This type of snail is mainly active at night. During the day, it shelters from the heat of the African sun under stones or leaves.

What?!?

It breeds really quickly, laying up to 200 eggs, five or six times a year. This means it has spread across the world very rapidly!

AUS USA
CHINA South Africa

Snails do not have ears. They FEEL the things we hear.

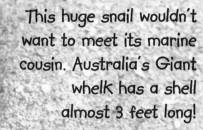

This huge snail wouldn't want to meet its marine cousin. Australia's Giant whelk has a shell almost 3 feet long!

BANANA SLUG

This extraordinary **slug** may look very similar to a **banana,** but is way **bigger**! It's not thought to be the world's **longest** slug, but it is probably the most **striking**.

I love slime!

Well, I think it looks nothing like me!

SLIME

Can you spot the difference?

Banana slugs produce a lot of slime. They use it to protect themselves, to help them move, to find a mate, and to keep moist.

Slugs are hermaphrodites, meaning they are both male and female.

19

Banana slugs have lots of tiny teeth—up to 27,000! Like sharks, they continuously regrow them. That's a lot of teeth to brush!

Like snails, slugs are molluscs, not insects. They have a foot, which is a large muscle that enables them to move, with the help of the foot's slime.

The banana slug is the official mascot of the University of Santa Cruz!

Eyes

Actual size: length 10 in

REAL-SIZE BUG

FACT FILE

Claim to bug fame:
The second largest slug

How big?
Up to 10 inches

What does it eat?
Mushrooms, leaves, decaying plants

Watch out. . . . **They are yellow and slimy, but not dangerous.**

Endangered?
No

Where in the world?
North America

CHINESE MANTIS

The **Chinese mantis** is one of the **largest** praying mantis species, with **females** growing up to 4 inches. Mantids are remarkable because their **forelegs** have **adapted** into spiky **"arms"** used to grab prey.

20

Females will sometimes even eat their mate!

Menu
House Special
Male Chinese
Mantis

FACT FILE

Claim to bug fame:
One of the largest praying mantids

How big?
Up to 4 inches

What does it eat?
Insects, sometimes even small frogs and birds

Watch out. . . . **They are ferocious predators but harmless to humans.**

Endangered?
No

Where in the world?
Asia, North America

Baby mantids are called nymphs, which hatch from eggs. They are said to look like miniature versions of their parents!

Can you see me?

Mantids are well camouflaged among leaves.

They have five eyes: two large ones and three smaller ones in between.

Actual size: length 4 in

Mantids can turn their triangular head 180 degrees to look behind themselves.

Mantids stay perfectly still until prey is within striking distance. Then they grab the prey so quickly that it's hard for humans to see!

REAL-SIZE BUG

Quick, run!

THE TOP SURVIVOR

Earthworm

DID YOU KNOW?
Worms are about 1,000 times stronger than people for their size!

Pull yourself together!

SIZE: Usually 3 in, but can grow much longer

DIET: Decaying plant matter

FROM: All places except frozen lands

SPECIAL SKILLS: The earthworm can survive being cut in two (but it doesn't become two worms).

Cockroach

DID YOU KNOW?
Cockroaches can hold their breath under water for up to 40 minutes!

SIZE: Usually around 1.5 in, but some grow much bigger

DIET: Anything

FROM: Worldwide

SPECIAL SKILLS: The cockroach can live for weeks without a head.

!!!

SO, WHO WINS THIS BUG BATTLE AS THE SUPREME SURVIVOR?
TURN TO PAGE 55 TO FIND OUT!

Color in these beetles
however you like!

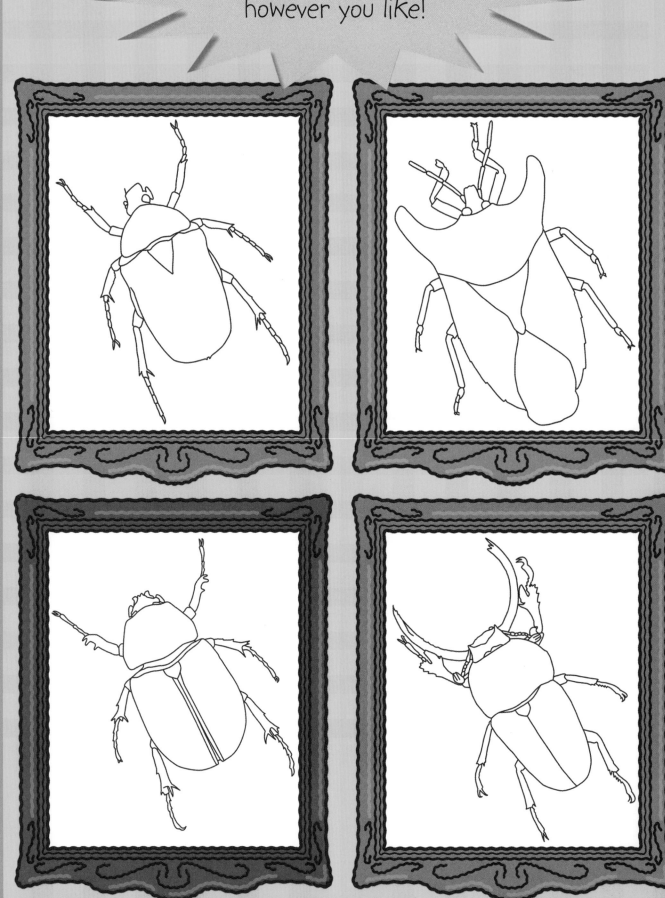

Can you find the missing puzzle piece? Choose from the three pieces below!

BUG BATTLE WINNERS

THE WORLD'S STRONGEST BUG

Officially the world's strongest animal, the Dung beetle is not just stronger for its size than any other bug, or any human— it's stronger than even an ox, or an elephant!

It's the DUNG BEETLE!

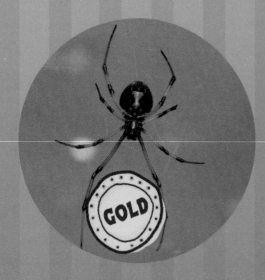

It's the
BLACK WIDOW
SPIDER!

THE MOST VENOMOUS BUG

The female Black Widow spider is one of the most venomous bugs in the world. It's rare, but her bite can kill a person. Her competitor, the Red-kneed tarantula, has a bite that's not much worse than a beesting.

THE SMELLIEST BUG

Not only is the Bombardier beetle's liquid spray boiling hot and smelly, it is also toxic. And it can spray up to 29 times in a row, directly toward a predator!

It's the
BOMBARDIER BEETLE!

THE HIGHEST JUMPER

The Froghopper is the high jump champion and has jumped as high as 28 inches. If a man (6 feet tall) were to jump the equivalent of a froghopper, he could get to the top of a 40-story building in one bound!

It's the FROGHOPPER!

A flea comes a close second. It can jump around 11 inches, but it is smaller, so it's almost as impressive. They both have in-built catapults that enable them to jump so high.

THE TOP SURVIVOR

Although it has been proven that cockroaches can last weeks without their head, the earthworm is the winner! It can not only survive being cut in half, it. . . .

- can go for three weeks without water.
- has been around longer than the dinosaurs.
- has survived four mass extinctions!

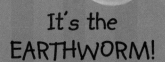

It's the EARTHWORM!

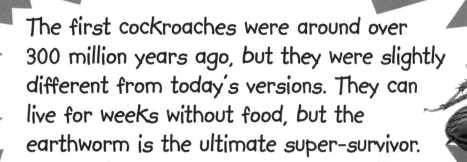

The first cockroaches were around over 300 million years ago, but they were slightly different from today's versions. They can live for weeks without food, but the earthworm is the ultimate super-survivor.

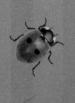

ANSWERS

Page 15

Page 43

Page 53

Pages 22 and 23 quiz: Who am I: 1. b), 2. b), 3. c), 4. a).

Pages 40 and 41 quiz: Odd one out: 1. b), 2. a), 3. a), 4. c), 5. c), 6. b) A caterpillar is a baby insect! 7. c), 8. b).

CREDITS

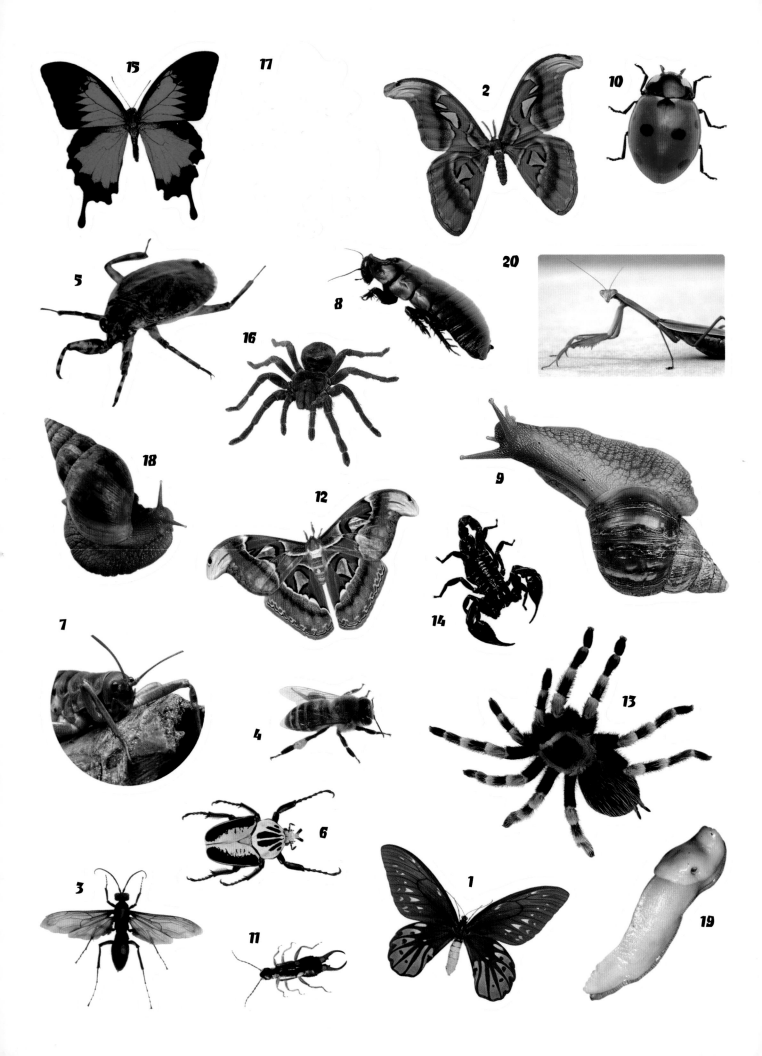

Add these fun stickers inside the book, or wherever you want!